The Life of AHPUN

IN HER MEMORY

Written by Shelley J. Evans

Illustrated by Rob Porter

For James + Jasmine ~ please enjoy my true story!

Shelley J Evans
1/5/21

PUBLICATION CONSULTANTS
We Believe In The Power Of Authors

PO Box 221974 Anchorage, Alaska 99522-1974
books@publicationconsultants.com—www.publicationconsultants.com

ISBN 978-1-59433-932-5

eBook 978-1-59433-9323-2

Library of Congress Catalog Card Number 2020908608

© 2020 Shelley J. Evans

—First Edition—

Illustrated by Rob Porter

Manufactured in the United States of America.

Acknowledgments

I give much credit and thanks to our daughter, Angelica Evans, Zookeeper/Enrichment Coordinator, Alaska Zoo; contributor to this book and its first editor; adventurer; lover or life, the environment, dogs (especially Marjorie, 14-year-old career-changed lab from Guide Dogs for the Blind) and all things animal! Angelica interned at the Zoo for 3 months one summer, when I visited and met the polar bears in person.

To my husband, Gary Evans, I give so much thanks and appreciation for being patient with me on this journey; listening to me read as I wrote and revised; sharing his opinions; encouraging me; and doing whatever it took to make this book happen, including his financial support.

Thank you to our daughters, Rachel Evans and Leah Evans, for their thoughts, editorial suggestions, and encouragement along the way.

Huge thanks to those family members and friends who so graciously responded to my friends funding letter, assisting with publishing and marketing costs.

Most importantly, I thank God for creating me, making me a poet, and always inspiring me with His creations in nature and His paintings in the sky. He fills my spirit with hope everlasting and the promise of eternity.

In spring of 1998, a fisherman, unaware,
Near Point Lay on Alaska's coast
Approached the den of a bear.
She charged him; he shot her
In self-defense, and then
Cautiously on hands and knees
He crawled inside the den.

There was a polar bear cub,
Orphaned and hungry, who
Would soon find herself at home
In the Alaska Zoo.

4

The cub's first night is a fond memory for the Zoo's director.
Knowing that bears rely upon their siblings and their mother,
And because she had no family, he chose to be her chap.
Speaking softly to her, she fell asleep snuggled on his lap.

This white bear was named Ahpun
(pronounced "Aw–poon") meaning snow
In the native language of Inupiaq Eskimo.
She truly was a fan of snow falling on the ground,
The full definition of her name which is profound.
Imagine Ahpun making snow angels while she rolled
On her back in fresh powder — what a sight to behold!

She weighed 31 pounds when she made her debut,
Crowned "Queen of the Snow Pile" and "Darling of the Zoo."
Zookeepers fed Ahpun, played with her, and gave her attention —
All the love they could offer as her mother would have given.
Even though the staff and keepers worked hard to be her "parents,"
They couldn't replace enrichment of another bear's presence.

A brown bear orphan, Oreo, came a short time after that;
And the bears were housed together sharing the same habitat.
Soon they were best buddies, batting toys and hugging each other;
Captivating staff and guests playing and sleeping together.
At times they would be frolicking and wrestling in tubs —
Five years in that environment, such very happy cubs.

The media was enthralled because unlike other zoos,
Two species of bears cohabiting was quite unique news.
A popular attraction, they co-starred in a video
That earned worldwide acclaim, "Playtime with Ahpun and Oreo."
A children's book was written, titled "Two Bears There,"
Of that dynamic duo's antics they would share.

They had such fun as playmates dazzling visitors at the Zoo;
Ahpun, the faster swimmer, Oreo, more agile of the two.
Fish were introduced in their pool; Ahpun caught and released them;
But Oreo was uncertain, afraid to swim with salmon.

Different personalities developed as they matured;
The brown bear was rambunctious, the polar bear more reserved.
In time, Oreo displayed aggression; Ahpun was aggravated;
And after a roaring, teeth-baring spat, the bears were separated.

Ahpun did not mind being alone and became more playful;
With Oreo out of sight, she'd swim for hours in the pool.
She'd dive into the water using her front legs as paddles,
Stroking freestyle gracefully, and her back legs were like rudders.

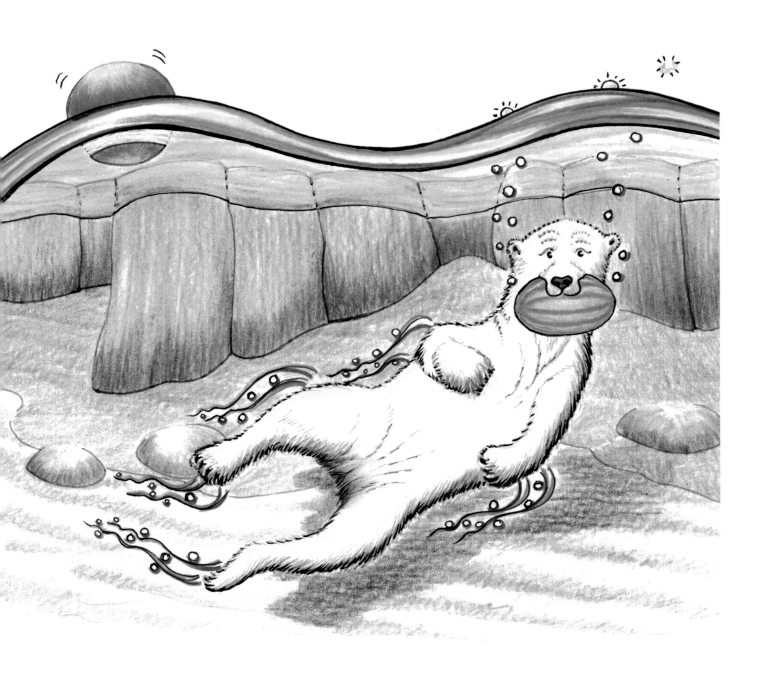

Enthusiastic swimmer, Ahpun loved to fish for salmon,
Halibut (her favorite treat), and in summer, watermelon.
Patiently she'd watch her keeper fix breakfast, hooligan
Which she loved but not their heads — she'd spit out every one!

Ahpun's visitors were not only of the human kind;
Ravens entered her exhibit for scraps of food to find.
Sweeping down from the sky to scavenge the den floor,
With a shrill alarm croaked the ravens, "We want more!"

Keepers nicknamed Ahpun "Hose–Snatcher" — she would lie in wait
And cunningly grab the hose when it slithered near her grate!
She'd watch for opportunities to mess with her zookeeper
And spy on construction workers, pouncing if they moved closer!

Oreo lived in a different part of the Alaska Zoo,
And Ahpun no longer had someone to give a bear hug to.
Eventually she felt the loneliness, being kept apart,
Until 2006 when Lyutyik came and captured Ahpun's heart.

He had resided at a zoo in St. Petersburg, Russia,
And moved to Anchorage from Sea World in Queensland, Australia.
He was brought to the Alaska Zoo from "The Land Down Under"
To be a partner for Ahpun; he became her "Boy Wonder"!

It was Lyutyik's desire to be with Ahpun right away,
But she was leery since Oreo had bullied her in play.
Four days later, the bears lay serenely close together,
A grated door between them playing footsies with each other.

Staff and guests watched the bears and patiently waited
For Ahpun and Lyutyik to get acclimated.
It wasn't long before they were romping around the den;
She seemed to accept him and enjoy having a new friend.
They would lounge side by side, groom the other's fur with claws,
Sprawled out on the ground of their enclosure touching paws.

Often the zookeepers observed her flirting with him,
But then she'd start acting fickle and go take a swim.
The pair was spotted mating; but alas, no baby bear
Ever arrived for Lyutyik and Ahpun to love and share.
It was unfortunate that she never conceived;
Everyone who cared about those two love–bears believed
She was beautiful and should have passed on her genes.
The making of a polar bear cub was in their dreams.

Through the years, she grew to 700 plus pounds easy
And was an iconic ambassador for her species.
Ahpun was chosen by Zoo staff to be the Prom Queen
And President the year before 2013.
She led the inner works of politics at the Zoo
Better than any other polar bear could ever do.

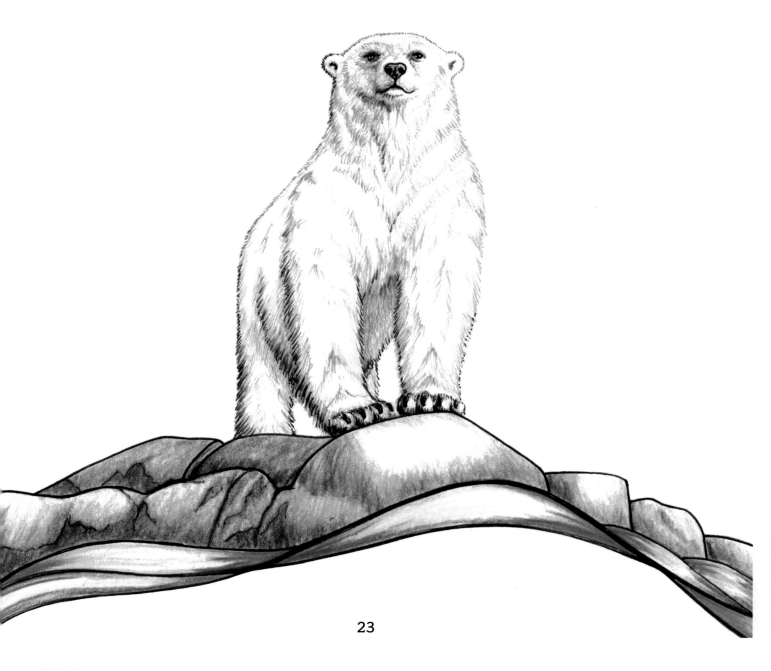

A truly remarkable creature who brought happiness to many,
Her life at the Zoo fostered education and understanding.
Clearly she was the people's star attraction for two decades,
And as such Ahpun enjoyed celebrating her birthdays.
During one of those parties she stood tall to reach and take
The top layer off her three-tiered, fish-packed, snow-iced cake!

The last day of 2017 Ahpun suddenly perished,
Devastating her community by whom she'd been so cherished.
The emotions of her loved ones were raw after they
Learned that their extraordinary "Pu–Bear" passed away.

Please, take a moment to eulogize Ahpun, if you will.
Visit the Alaska Zoo where her memory lives on still.
She'll always be remembered with joy and happiness.

Smart, gentle, mellow, gorgeous

AHPUN

you'll be missed.

Angelica Evans

Glossary of Terms

acclaim – public praise

acclimated – to adapt to or get used to something or someone new

agile – able to move quickly and easily

aggravated – feeling annoyed, irritated

aggression – violent behavior, forcefulness

ambassador – representative

antics – amusing or silly behavior

approached – came near in distance

attraction – an entertainment offered to the public

captivating – holding people's attention

captured – attracted attention

cautiously – carefully

chap – man, friend

charged – rushed aggressively toward someone or something in attack

cherished – adored, loved

cohabiting – living together

community – group of people living in the same place

conceived – got pregnant

co-starred – appeared with another star

creature – an animal

cunningly – in a clever way

dazzling – impressive, incredible

debut – first time in public

decade – a period of ten years

definition – meaning

desire – strong feeling of wanting or wishing for something

devastating – causing terrible upset

developed – caused to grow and become more mature

different – not the same

displayed – showed

duo – a pair of people or things

dynamic – full of energy

emotions – feelings

enclosure – pen, yard

enrichment – improving the quality of life

enthralled – delighted, fascinated

enthusiastic – having or showing enjoyment, excitement

environment – the area where something lives

Eskimo – an indigenous person living in Alaska; the language spoken by such person

eulogize – praise highly as a memorial after someone's death

eventually – after some time

exhibit – place where bears are housed

extraordinary – above and beyond what is expected

fickle – changing behavior, flighty

flirting – teasing

fostered – helped, assisted

freestyle – front crawl swim stroke

frolicking – playing, moving about cheerfully, energetically

genes – inherited from parents

gorgeous – dazzlingly beautiful

gracefully – in an attractively elegant way

groom – brush, comb

habitat – the natural home or environment of an animal

human – relating to people

iconic – relating to an icon, symbolic of an idol or hero

imagine – visualize, see in the mind's eye

introduced – put in place for the first time

Inupiaq – an Eskimo person living in northwestern Alaska, the language of such person

language – method of communication

leery – uncertain

lounge – lie down in a relaxed way

mating – breeding

matured – aged, grew older

media – the main means of mass communication, news

mellow – easygoing, good-natured

native – associated with birthplace

nicknamed – gave a humorous name instead of the real name

observed – watched

opportunities – chances

orphaned – made parentless through the death of parents

paddles – short poles with broad blades at the ends to move through water

passed away – died

patiently – accepting delays without becoming annoyed

31

perished – died

personalities – qualities that formed the nature of the bears

politics – activities associated with governing an area

popular – liked, admired, or enjoyed by many people

presence – being there

profound – wise, clever, insightful

rambunctious – rowdy, wild, unruly

raw – painful

released – set free, let go

rely – depend on with full trust

remarkable – amazing, wonderful

replace – take the place of

reserved – quiet, private

resided – lived in

rudders – flat pieces of wood or other material used to steer in the water

scavenge – search for and collect things from discarded waste

self-defense – protect oneself

separated – moved apart

serenely – in a calm, peaceful manner

shrill – high-pitched and piercing

siblings – brothers and/or sisters

slithered – moved with a twisting, snake-like motion

species – a group of similar animals

sprawled – lying down with legs stretched out

star attraction – celebrity or hero type crowd-pleaser

stroking – moving arms and legs to swim

suddenly – quickly, without warning

sweeping – moving swiftly and smoothly

three-tiered – three layered

unaware – not knowing

uncertain – not sure of something, unclear

unfortunate – unlucky

unique – being the only one of its kind, unlike anything else, special

worldwide – throughout the world, global, international

zookeeper – an animal attendant who works in a zoo